JANGLE

JANGLE

POETRY
BY
LISA
BUSCANI

TIA CHUCHA PRESS, CHICAGO

ACKNOWLEDGMENTS:

"Regina"was first performed in Circa 1992 at the Cabaret Metro, Chicago, IL; "Elvis" and "These boots are made for walkin'" were first performed in Milly's Orchid Show at The Park West, Chicago, IL; "A prayer" was first performed at The Rants and Prayers Show, part of the Outsider Cabaret at Lower Links, Chicago, IL; "Cab addict," "Barefoot in the city," "Hemingway afternoon," "Jangle," "Temper," "Counting," and "Miss Mary Mack," were first performed in Too Much Light Makes the Baby Go Blind at the Stage Left Theater, The Live Bait Theater and the Neo-Futurarium, Chicago, IL. All other pieces were first performed in the Uptown Poetry Slam at the Green Mill Lounge, Chicago, IL.

Thanks to Marc Smith, who said yes from the beginning; to The Touchstones, the women I want to be when I grow up: Paula Killen, Cin Salach, Patricia Smith, and Jenny Magnus; to the Neo-Futurists, who help me think it all through: Ayun, Heather, Karen, Spencer, Betsy, Dave, Greg K., Phil, Greg A., Tim, Ted and Adrian; to Luis Rodriguez for hounding me; to my illustrator and hulking one-man entourage, John Jerard: Baby, you can clean my pool; to Mom, Dad, Pete, Elyn and Julie for understanding even when I didn't; and to Bruce Neal: You are one nasty, angular hunk o'vision, mister, and I love you very much.

Second printing, 1993

Cover Art: "Barking Heart," by John Jerard, based on the poem, "Right."

Illustrations for "Clown," "Troller," "Home," "Jangle" and "Drive" by John Jerard

Design: Jane Kremsreiter
Typesetting: Susan Dühl

Printed in the United States

ISBN 0-9624287-8-7

Library of Congress Catalog Card Number: 92-64246

TIA CHUCHA PRESS
A Project of the Guild Complex
PO Box 476969
Chicago, IL 60647
312-252-5321

Distributed by:
Inland Book Company
140 Commerce Street
East Haven, CT 06512
203-467-4257

This project partially supported by grants from the City of Chicago Department of Cultural Affairs, Office of Fine Arts, the Illinois Arts Council, and the National Endowment for the Arts.

Stuff the head
with all such reading
as was never read:
for thee explain a thing til all men
doubt it
and write about it,
Goddess, and about it.

ALEXANDER POPE

CONTENTS

▶ Girly girl,
She who was he as she,
Girly girl walked it,
that full, undulating runway walk
that walk of spine and arrogance,
the walk that said
water
and
fuck you.

REGINA

Her hair fell into a careful, careless curl,
the acid that forced it to relax
a momentary inconvenience.
Her breasts were padded with wishes and pictures,
saying nurture and wonder,
saying lifeline and spotlight,
saying comfort and fortune.
Her firm, manly ankles
alternated between best feature
and biggest give-away.
The tips of her spikes
bit into a world only happy to bite back.
The hem
of her tasteful Chanel ensemble
kissed her mid-thigh because
honey
everything should.

She was just this side of parody.
Brighter and sharper
than any woman could be.
She was like those women
who weren't but were,
dressed in dreams,
shot in shadows
and looking up from under.
And no, she wasn't a woman
but she knew what woman was:
life's finest detail,
an unfailing rhythm,

a gift to be opened and peeled away lightly.

And she walked Newtown Broadway,
land of overpriced bars and bad coffeehouses,
land of urbane trash and Cubs fans
shaking their pin heads in disbelief
as she walked by.
She walked it,
queen for a day,
all day every day,
not to the manner born
but to the manner borrowed.

And when they spat the word "faggot"
like bad aftertaste,
when the word "faggot"
slid from under its rock
to block her path,
when the word "faggot" sneered from the mouths
of minds too small to hold anything else,
she called on the goddesses
that she prayed to daily
for the patience to outlast it,
for the strength to endure it,
for the style to rise above.

Marlene,
hear me
Josephine,
hear me
Ms. Davis,
hear me
Joan Crawford,
hear me
Marilyn,
hear me
Mahalia,
hear me
Grace Jones,
hear me
Madonna,
hear me

And she raised her square shoulders,
and she thrust her rough chin forward,
and she executed a perfect

1950s B-movie pivotal moment turn
and said,
WHAT
WOULD
YOU
KNOW
ABOUT
GLAMOUR
MOTHAFUCKA!

And it gave her great joy
to watch their amazed faces fall,
to hear air sputter in search of retort,
to smell the progression of fear to caution to respect.

Girly girl
she who was he as she,
Girly girl walked it.
Long live the queen.

▶ The world is pushing,
the world is shoving,
the world is grasping for rung or pole,
the world is sharing sweat and breath,
the world is stepping-to-the-back-of-the-bus-please-people,
the world is closing in.

But not on me.
I am above the world.
I have chosen
(how I love that verb and its fat finality)

C AB ADDICT

to take a cab.

Cabs make me automatically regal.
Someone out there somewhere
exists solely to serve me
and will whisk me
through the clogged arteries of our flabby metropolis
to a destination that no one else will share.
Fuck community,
I deserve curbside service.

Privacy is so soft,
so quiet.
The world of the cab is
a world full of classical music on Sunday mornings,
the mouths of men after successful sex,
art museums during the Superbowl.
And the voices of the cab drivers
reflect and revere that intimacy
cheeks to pillow
cream to coffee.

"Racine and Montrose?
Sure.
You know, it's supposed to snow . . .
lips pillow day
Time sweet gift yellow hold . . .
you know?"

Yes . . .

"So I says to the wife, I says . . .
'Dream brush wonder hug silhouette

4

Days kissing breath shiver silk.
Question cellophane dish and cream.'
Am I right, or am I right?"

Yes, o-h-h y-e-e-e-s-s-s . . .

And as we glide through time,
the calm of it all is enough to consider,
just consider mind you,
moving to the suburbs.

► Hugging up a
shall we say,
Rubenesque thigh,
I donned yet another tightly woven layer
in an attempt to hard-pack myself into credibility.
It wasn't working.

A silkier bond,
that's for sure,
a yoke you take for the sake of lines,
a clinging, hazy refinement that says

L EGS

I am polished.
I am defined.
I am synthetic.

But just this day,
the wide, high sun
brought such personal borders
too, too close.
A thousand, itchy, shimmering strands
cutting me,
binding me, wrapping me in sheerest undertones
to roles that I could never mold myself into.
Cramming me into limits,
amazed at how such things
always work their way to your crotch.
Reminding me
how I pour myself
day in, day out
into a one-size-fits-all-life
hypnotized,
categorized,
illogically alphabetized A, B, C, Q. . .

Looking down to the breakthrough.

A chink in the armor,
a rip in the net,
usually met with a flurry of oaths and polish,
now seen as safe passage to . . .
Anarchy!

Now as bond breaking,
now as sentence ending,
now as a sucker for an unraveling,
I am woman, watch me rip!

Microscopic threads pop dissension
as I rip away feminine mystake!
Running, webbing, snaring, tearing,
until no cross-cage is as it was
or ever will be again!

Spent
staggering through steamy streets,
heading for that mecca of retail,
numbers almost Korannical,
Seven-Eleven,
What-ho, Mohammed!
No nonsense here.
Let us begin again.

Troller

▶ The wife's not home,
or the wife's not,
or he's a blue, blue boy
with a wet, eclectic mouth,
or he just can't stand to hear himself
slam back like that,
or they're all, they're all,
well
they are.

TROLLER

And that's fine.
Hell, a spasm is the next best thing
to actually being there.
But you forget, I'm here.
Not pious per se,
but much too confused
by the politics of gift
to benefit from the cold reality
of cash.

Please excuse the noise
which garbles out as anger.
I know that strangled hormones
can transform bare face and sweatpants
into baby's delight.
But you see
nobodies
every day
score points on me.
Heavy-handed, thick-tongued half shells
whose glazed eyes
I can honestly stare into and say
oh, fuck you.
This is my day,
my time,
my step fuller,
my mind leaner,
my mouth the best of every goddamn thing you know.
These assholes are winning.
And the chance to say no
to an unconsented squeal

to an unsolicited bend and spread
is a little victory
that I will have.

So strip your gears
and anything else you damn well please
but this ample curve and flawed gait
walk where they will.
These hands wrap their magic
around the freedom of choice.

The choice is made,
the answer's no,
fuck off.

► You can't walk barefoot in the city.
Or you can,
if you're willing to chance . . .

The city covers its base
with things that stay with you,
with dog shit, with trash, with glass.

But still, you'll go where you'll go.

BAREFOOT IN THE CITY

They say that the foot
is the soul of the body.
No pun intended.
The center of everything is felt at the bottom.

The heat we've covered with concrete
is still with us.
We feel what's living and vital
underneath a face that would destroy us.

It's amazing what we'll do for warmth.

In Washington, DC, a local businessman attempted to provide shelter for that city's homeless population by manufacturing and distributing prefabricated sheds. Authorities removed them, claiming that the sheds were unfit housing.

▶ It's the roughest we have,
unfinished grain
slapdashed together
at one hundred bucks a pop.

If you try to know it,
run your hands over it,
pieces of it stay with you
bleeding permanence.

B OX

So show it for what it is:
cursory home.
And don't let it under your skin.

The door swings shut on second-hand hinges.
There is something infinitely merciful
about an object that stands
between you and the draw
that drags back a lifetime.

Here, time and space are your own.
Add that to rheumy memory
and you've summed up current worldly assets.
Here, the difference between restless
and unable to rest
is not a matter of semantics.

It's a water-tread slide
with a pull
a stretch
a thin-fingered grasp
an infinite tip of the chin
as you flounder over levels
that show you daily who's boss.

Hold still and hear your heart beat street.
Move on, move on
Hear your muscles pop disapproval.
Move on, move on
Hear old bones scream for downtime.
Move on, move on

And when the door swings open,
claim flight as title.
12   Again.

▶ Spangle and wiggle,
Girl-child chic,
We're a backstreet DEtroit upgrade
clocking timepiece moves.
Hear us and you say "girl"
with three R's and a honey slide
That's what Mr. Gordy says.

I AM THE FOURTH SUPREME

A few bars into us
and little girls run for brush mikes
and bounce along to a rough-boy beat.
We're the baby love tasty enough
for general sensibilities,
not just the less profitable homie market
That's what Berry says.

But Diana,
A drop-eyed shark smile behind four-foot lash,
Diana's pushing front lines,
Diana's pushing shine,
Diana's pushing Berry.

But we push on.
Back beat in a negative arrangement,
black matter on an all-white image,
backing away from an ethnic roar
as the silver gathers.

► Day-o staggers home,
gin-drooling a calypso jig,
shuffling an old, addled ska,
bemoaning what this dancing has become.

Once, in warmer times,
these beats kept him glorious,
palm kisses left him breathless,
roll-rocking reckless in appetite's haze.

TROPICO

He stretched himself wild,
fed his rhythms to the lion's breath,
cleansed himself in syncopation,
raining full and sweet and free in the den.

But now, in this place,
with its pin-point mewling sun,
damp smiles and cast down glances,
the dancing is so desperate, so tired.

Nights he scuffs frenzy,
celebrating his tenacity,
that he still breathes in this jagged glass teeming,
stepping fast among manic blood angle.

He flails a heat pulsed swirl,
curls and sweats hard teeth-lined snaps
because he will not give easy to this place;
not he, the day-kissed one, the lion's child.

And he shimmies tatters,
drags a frayed, ragged soca,
molds a lover's grip with gray,
and faces west
for warmer breezes.

▶ Firm with years of affirmation
that greatness was mine,
I swaggered down to the South Loop
to grab some good for my two shoes.

I met the politely pressed from the 'burbs,
more servants than served, which was good.
Holiday catharsis, I guess,
catholics all.

And as we braced in our cool charity,

ELECTRICAL WORKERS UNION HALL: THANKSGIVING, 1987

suddenly, there was this sour wall
of weather-beaten black and khaki.
They looked like art students,
but their haircuts were less expensive.
The day's kings and queens had arrived
and we waxed domestic.

We were motivated,
and the processed turkey circles flew.
But it was an assembly line kindness,
"Hello-how-are-you-have-a-meal-hit-the-road."
And I knew if I saw them tomorrow,
I wouldn't remember them,
and I probably wouldn't even try.
Now that's holiday magic.

And then toward the end,
There was a woman in a red ski jacket
and she was in from Schaumburg to pick up her Cub Scouts.
She was me.
Or she was down from Winnetka with baked goods.
She was me.
Or she was in from Lake Forest, curious.
She was me.

And she sat down,
And she took a meal
And she ate it like she knew what it meant.

And the maginot exploded.
All glistening guarantees fly blown
and we, she and I,

so new in chosen roles,
could have easily exchanged.

Up until then it had been glamorous, perverse fun.
Up until then, I was Lisa of Assisi.
Elbow to elbow with fellow men,
but an arm's length away.

But she,
so with me,
of me,
in me,
it was much too close.

Lessons learned.
Teenagers who dallied with oldsters,
having known its face, mind and memory
will probably see poverty as somewhat less grody.

And me, I'll be a repeat offender
Because, in all selfishness,
I'll be working for me.

▶ He snipped and clipped
and brushed it back,
but it just kept growing.
Kudzu, had he known it,
would not have been as fearless.

He waged a constant war,
for often it covered him,
 stifling and smothering.
And just when he thought he had it
shaped into a liveable cut,

THE BARBER

the French Jew arrived
and demanded answers.

So he did what he always did
for the last 45 years.
He cut the Jew's hair,
and he tried to find the words.

Yes, he had known.
No, he didn't understand it,
but God has his plans.
Well, the people went in,
you know
and they did not come out.
And that smell.
You couldn't forget that smell.

They came to him and others
in August of 1940.
They said that they were streamlining the operation
and that they needed his services.
The black and red they wore
denoted the fire awaiting refusal.
They needed no arms.

They drove him to the camp,
and took him to a long, grey room
and gave him dull, rusty tools.
And in came the women.
Shorn of all,
this last slap was personal.

Off, they said.

Cut it all off,
and sort it into piles
according to color.
Most of the women knew what was coming
and that he was preparation.
And he tried to do it nice,
to give them one last beauty.
But the Gestapo demanded faster madness
and he stripped them of ornamentation as quickly as he could.

And if he hurt them,
he apologized.
And if they cried, he lied
and said that he was sure everything would be alright.
God has his plans.
Because that's what you say to a dying woman.

And when they left,
he looked at what they left him,
life reduced to byproduct
And he wondered what God if any had a plan like that.

Why, asked the Jew
and he cut.
Why, pleaded the Jew
and he snipped.
Why, bleated the Jew
and he trimmed.

Why
and he cut
Why
and he snipped
Why
and he trimmed
because it just kept growing.

Clown

► My boy
fly boy
Sky
stood on the platform and waited for the train.
In the season of time
at the time of night
when the fetid air
and lack of light
remind you that
the world is hell
and you are alone.

C LOWN

But he was not.
The man slicked his hair back like
fake teddy boy glory,
wore a grin as sticky
as greasepaint,
groomed his full black moustache,
the talisman of butch prowess,
cinched his ever-expanding waistline
in a bloated line of power,
and kept his mind tight.

Had he ever considered the clown?
the man asked Sky
that the right face could be so basic
in any occupation.
That laughter hitches in the throat with no notice,
the simple, delightful element
of surprise. . .
Clown faces ran from the man's paint brush often
and would Sky like to see?
The man thrust a sunny hand forward,
drew up a big-sky stance,
opened his smile wide
and introduced himself as
John Wayne Gacy.

Sky stepped back.
Stepped back from possible futures,
sidestepped to the ready shell he kept
for friendly strangers,
stepped apart from the boys

who wore their blood in their pout,
who could reconcile a moment of sex
with a lifetime of survival,
who had tasted just enough bad days
to pan hope from the attentions
of a sad, fat, old queen,
whose throats circled small in the onset of horror,
whose lips parted with
the force of constricted wind,
whose screams raced under
and above their skin,
whose eyes were as flat
as the beat they lost.
Thirty-three boys,
wrapped in shadow,
thirty-three boys,
bathed in freeze frame,
thirty-three boys,
lying soft in their blood.

Sky stepped back.
No, man
no.

► When I was a child,
the word could be counted
on one hand:
to home
face to home.
Breathe and bend with the constant.
Know its scent,
wait for that warmth.
Home will bring you in,
catch you up
and hold the rhythm of your only haven.

BASE

For the foreign step,
save a downcast eye
and no time ever.
To home
face to home.

But what when home blackens?
Heart's lifeblood slacks and congeals.
What when the hearth burns too high
and forges the bonds that tie you to your worst night?

When the eyes grow flat
and the lids bend to save them from light.
when nostrils cave out for air,
when the mouth razors white
and cuts questions you've never heard
in a pace that assaults you,
in a voice choked thick and wet,
and the jaw clenches in unbalanced authority,
and the fist and fingers move harder and faster,
and the whole body stands in a screaming proximity
that you haven't dealt with
ever.
When home is gone.
When time is old.
When hope is a far, small light.
Who will you smile for then?

In March of 1988, a Birmingham, AL, man was convicted of molesting an eleven-year-old girl. As part of his sentence he was required to tape a confession of his crime, and to make a formal apology to the girl and her parents.

▶ Roll 'em.
And now, by court order,
stand before them
and hand them
the blond-haired, blue-eyed Aryan line.
See if they bite.
I don't think so.

CONFESSION

Tell them of the lies,
the raw denial,
even though eleven-year-olds
can't dream of such invasions
unless they have to.

Tell them of the soft,
the young arch,
And how easy it is in your mind
to change the eyes of fear and pain
to love and lust,
and make her feel
the need,
the need,
Jesus, the need.

Tell her now.
And make it good.
Because in five years
when she firms and points,
finds her smooth,
and deals with these behaviors in choice,
she'll need it.

Tell her
that she wasn't such a special pout.
She wasn't bad
as much as she was
logistically correct,
someone to have a hold over
at the right place
right time.

Tell her
that she was just another direction.
That we all fall,
don't we,
and you went down deeper than most.

Tell her now.
And make it good.
In five years,
you'd better hope it's enough.

And cut, wrap, print.

▶ You did not mess with Big LaQuita.
The middle of her brow split in deep furrow,
her eyes winced,
pained in half-slash,
her nostrils folded out in horns of anger,
her mouth
black and down,
wowling like a hot cat,
her hands clasped tightly
demanding that she be with

FEEDING BIG LAQUITA

what she was without.
It was feeding time.
The girl was hungry.

LaQuita's lips taught me power and need.
The pink life of it;
A full, wet hold.
Drawing back and hard on the nipple
with a clean, tender pull.
She cried for just that one thing,
food
in large, liquid quantities.
Lots of kids in the center
that's all that would please them.
They ate constantly, ravenously,
remembering frantically that they might not
have this again,
mouths in filling motion,
keeping the ghosts at bay,
the holes to a blue murmur.
I understood that.
Food is fast satisfaction.
Everything else
takes at least five minutes.

LaQuita knew that.
LaQuita's lips knew that.
And when you put the bottle in LaQuita's mouth,
her lips locked on the nipple
with a finite, military precision,
like a sharpshooter on his life's target.

As able armies of bubbles marched doubletime
to the great unknown,
as air said its final farewell,
as the captain downed her ship.
It was feeding time.
LaQuita was commander-in-chief.

Big LaQuita was the ugliest child
I'd ever seen in my life.
Stone homely.
She was six months old with a face of a
55-year-old domestic worker
after a particularly hard day,
and one look to that woman's hands
shows even her skin is voting to leave.
And I figured that a face like that
in a life like hers
wouldn't cut many breaks,
so I spent as much time with her
as I could.

Which wasn't much.
At the center,
time was as tight as a fat man's waist band,
with so much more left to cover.
There were babies everywhere.
Light, sweet smiles
in cribs,
in bassinets,
in walkers,
Always with an open face and an empty hand
and blank spaces when you looked at their past
and their future.

The center was a place for the waiting
and the weighted.
Young mothers with no plan,
hearts waning on the sound,
of slamming doors,
suns setting so casually
you could miss their colors
if you didn't look twice.
They came there because their backs were scarred
with the marks of all the walls
they'd been pushed to,
one denial toppled a hundred more

dominoes of option,
failing, failing, failing.

Most of the babies I worked with
had already been taken away
from their parents,
people so hazed that one more loss
just shaded them further.
Some were born high and dirty,
a picture that doesn't fit with birth.
A drug loses all of its underhanded humor
when it flows through the veins of a baby.
When their backs are stiff as boards
and they're always cold,
and they won't be held
and they're always crying.
Their fights were so brittle,
their hearts skipped so easily,
we attached electronic beepers
that would scream at us
when connections were cut.

I lulled into the center
with nothing but time.
It was bighearted and ragged
full of just enough to go round.
Second-hand rockers,
institutional blankets,
just getting on,
just getting over.

I dripped in and figured,
cool.
Dry a tear, pat a head,
and that will toss me
into the big house salad
of the great garbanzo bean above.
And all of a sudden,
Me
wet-spangled gypsy girl,
Me
the consummate summer sometime thing,
Me
goddess of amble and meander,
I paced their clock.

I was the even beat they needed.

Nap at one, changed at four, fed at 4:15.
And I tell you
it felt good,
looking down instead of out.
If you've ever rocked a baby to sleep
it's a breath.
A free, deep breath,
completely unencumbered.
And those don't come along too often.

Tyrone was my first diaper.
Heaven help the virgin of the bassinet.
Tyrone was beautiful.
He had the biggest smile,
the biggest eyes,
and the biggest load in his pants
I had ever seen.
I stripped off his diaper
and marveled at the fact that
regardless of what color child it comes from
baby shit
is the strangest shade of green.
I fumbled around our new-found intimacy
and tried to wipe him
as the towelette shredded into
the filthy crevices of his skin,
as he wriggled like a worm
facing death by trout,
as I tried to put a newborn's diaper
on a two-year-old butt.
Finally,
frazzled and covered in his excrement,
I looked at Tyrone and said,
Honey,
I'm so sorry.
I'm new at this.
And he looked up at me
and just smiled as if to say,
that's okay.
I can wait.

Many of those kids waited a long time
for their parents to get their shit together.
It didn't always happen.

LaQuita's mom was so high on a visit,

she picked up the wrong baby.
Amillionara's mom fed her cut-up hot dogs
at eight months.
When we brought Amillionara back to strained peas,
she was pissed.
It was like she'd been demoted on the food chain.
Amillionara was as close
to imperious
as a baby could get.
She liked to get a running start
in her walker,
glide across the day room,
bark you on the shin
and look up as if to say
ExCUSE me.

Amillionara's mom bolted
from the adolescent floor upstairs.
She was pregnant again
and it had gotten too tight,
all of it.
So she ran dirty,
it was always dirty here,
no matter what you did,
so she gave over and ran with it.
Ran light,
she was good at it once.
And tried to find the place
where she could live small again,
with her girl's dreams
The way it was before the sidelines
of arch and angle turned her way.
Amillionara was our guest for a little longer.

Beyond a clean dry butt
and a steady fix of formula,
the babies asked for home,
or something of that anchor.
But no amount of bright primary colors
could mend the flaws they came with.
Home is something much heavier,
at least as I knew it,
and we just didn't have that pull.

Which isn't to say that we didn't try.

The ladies of the day room,
with their meaty, full-hipped swagger,
couldn't love those kids enough.
They were spat on,
shat on,
drooled on,
puked on,
and met each natural disaster
with something easy like
Girl
I love you anyway.
The ladies' pace
knew no surprises.
World weary,
they were fierce and solid
and necessarily distant.
No turns unhinged them.
They knew what was behind most of the doors.
There was no anger in their past
and no fear in their future.

Hey girl,
Girl,
Hey boy,
Boy,
Yes you, Shorty
I think I'm talking to you.
We're going to take what the world gives us
before it's taken back in dust,
Yes
tip its chin up and teach it to look skyward,
Yes
feed it with the only milk,
Yes
put it on its own feet,
Yes
in grace,
Yes
in love,
Yes
and help it find the time and place to breathe.

Olympia frightened me even before I knew
There were no tears
but she cried all the time,

keeping her release at hand
because she was one of those children
who needed it.
When you held her, she clung to you.
You could take your hands away
and she'd still be there.
She wore these tight, padded
nylon medical pants and
they were difficult to put on and remove.
A nun asked me once to help her change Olympia,
she had wet herself.
As we rolled the pants to Olympia's knees
I saw small, raised circular scars
on the back of her butt and thighs,
and before I knew it,
before I knew to bend and protect
the girl from her own reality,
before I knew to take what I saw into me
and let the silence be the better for everybody,
I muttered,
Jesus, it looks like they burned her ass with an iron.

Well, of course they had.
I couldn't know that life.
Ever.

The nun looked at me
as if I were god's own
dull-eyed, froth-lipped idiot,
where was my sense,
the child didn't need reminders
and my, my, my,
but it was hard to get good help these days.
She rolled up the pants
and carried Olympia off to bed.

Yolanda was wilted.
Wilted.
Anyone would in the heat of her life,
so she did.
She was terribly burned on her legs, arms and back.
Her parents were freebasing when the house caught fire.
They forgot she was there.
She wore an entire bodysuit
made of the same tight nylon material Olympia wore.
Most of her pain was over,

and she was healing,
But it took a lot to ride this thing.
The push that gets you over
the red crest
comes dear,
and Yolanda was tired.
But the ladies of the day room kept calling,
kept begging for a smile,
kept reminding her who she was,
who she'd always be,
pretty girl,
pretty girl.
They knew there is more than one way
to be a pretty girl
and Yolanda had to find it.
So they kept calling down to the diamond,
to the ray that would set her above it all,
to the shine that would push her beyond
what she was to the eye.
They kept at it,
culling up a smile
a salve of tone and contact,
a balm of touch, attention, repetition,
Hey, pretty girl . . .

And we watched her unfold.
She broke away from the off-mark
focus of an unknown point
and looked at us now.
Her eyes filled out from her constant wince
and stopped bracing themselves for more pain.
Her voice, which she shut off
for the silence of survival came back
and she sang to herself,
and when she was wet or hungry,
we knew it.
The ladies weren't surprised.
Kids come back like that.
All new breaks and dayliving,
all first light and fresh chances.
Their time was so new, you couldn't jade them
against themselves.
It took the access of a parent to do that.

And I fell into it,

like the rhythm of blood,
like the taste for skin,
like the peace of age,
my eyes and ears attuned to the nuance
of their small needs.
like breathing
the feeding
in
the changing
out
the sleeping
in
the playing
out
We found our biological, chronological balance
and held it as best we could.
Until
the unexpected tugged at my pant leg.
Until
control wriggled from my hands to a busy thoroughfare.
Until
fear cloaked my shoulders as ragged as low fashion.
A beeper went off
Its thin red whine not quite the magnitude
needed for impending doom.
A beeper went off
Screaming for some action,
warning of lost order,
wailing of pain and loss
A beeper went off
and there was no escaping
the inevitable,
the inalienable,
the undeniable,
I had fucked up.
Their trust was wasted,
their gift was squandered,
and I rushed to the crib
with a slack mouth and eulogy mind,
with cracked shells and ending credits,
with flat eyes and past tense,
and look down and look down and look down
to find he

She

looking up at me,
young lord of tabula rasa saying,
What's the ruckus, bub?

The beeper went off by accident.
The baby had pulled away
or turned in its sleep,
or done something natural,
because babies do.

And I thought:
Saved, this time.
Saved, for now.
And I prayed the world would catch them like that
in the future.

▶ And we'll never find happiness!
No, never!
And we'll never get to Moscow!
And Irina's crying again . . .

And there's never enough vodka!
No, never!
And little Masha's drowning!
And Irina's crying again . . .

CHEKOVIAN DEPRESSION

Ah Sergei, how I loved you once.
The autumn leaves, golden in their sadness!
Olga, you were so lovely once.
The spring buds, green in their naive futility!

When! When does the pain subside?
Ivan Ivanovitch has hung himself, you know!
Little Masha's on fire now,
And Irina's crying again . . .

The summer smothers each
in its godless communist heat!
It's true about Alexei Petrovitch,
he died of a broken heart!
The winter clutches each
in its unrelenting Lenin-like grip!
never, never to ease!
Little Masha,
buried alive,
Somebody choke that bitch Irina,
and life,
life is death!
Death!
Death!
And thick-soled boots!

▶ When Elvis died,
I hid from the rain
underneath an aluminum table in my basement.
Radio waves hung
muzzling about the tornado,
a black, angry funnel cloud
coiling our way.
The air outside was perched on a moment.
We knew.

E LVIS

And in between bated weather-breath,
the newsman pined for Elvis.
For street-smart flannel baggies,
for self-conscious karate suits,
Las Vegas' reason to viva.

They said the boy gave out and over.
The moves don't roll no more,
the angles fatted in caricature.
The sneer bent back from impudence
to sheer, pure disgust.

A heart can only hold that for so long.

But just as light must fly forever,
just as sound sings beyond the hearing,
just as love lives without the lover,
what he was
must go somewhere.

And in the storm's eye,
I saw him:
His soul circling close to the vortex,
holding elements as his own,
enfolded in a different grace.
Roiling high above the earth,
flying finally;
riding with the wind's rage,
caged in walls of bad weather,
hotter than a frustrated sock hop.

It was

Elvis
hips spinning on a ragged angle,
Elvis
mouth molded slow to the Southern vowel,
Elvis
dyed-black, down-home, uptown,
Elvis
Picking the world up
and slamming its ass back down,
just to mix it up,
just a little,
because that,
my friends,
is what a bad boy's for.

Gone, man.
Solid gone.

▶ From the back of the box,
she and I were beauteous cruel.
Staring down upstart starlets,
dealing out round after round Of Human Bondage
to an impossibly sappy Leslie Howard,
or nobly bearing the pain of fate
like the cinematic bluebloods we were.
In all, we were one long luscious.

Able to leap short, Jewish movie moguls
in a single bound,

MOTHER GODDAMN: BETTE DAVIS, 1987

she was nobody's sweetmeat.
In the 1940s, any woman offering even
the most figurative of fuck-offs was a big deal.
That she could break from the stable and profit
was bigger still,
and I drank her in
as I looked for a model to fill me.

On Oscar night,
they announced her name over and over in promo
because they know that legends rate.
And when the moment was right,
in the appropriate flourish of color and light
the grande dame made her entrance . . .

And I saw aging's most graceless face.
Such rich ripe shrunken to half that splendor,
swaddled in a bag dress,
wearing a wig two sizes too blonde.
The rumors were right,
the stroke had not been kind.
It took the killer claw from her eyes
and jammed it around her mouth.

And she babbled on of Babylon,
spewing what she knew to anyone who would listen,
it was a terrible slice of real-life Gollum,
even uglier than colorization.

That is not the ending that I paid to see.
That is not what happened to Baby Jane.

A woman like her shouldn't know
the whimper of physical indignity.
A woman like her should brash endless.
A woman like her should leave this life
having pronounced the earth terminally
dirth of chic.
And with light high,
in that patented bad-ass bitch goddess banter,
announce "What a dump!"
and flounce over to the next simply celestial soiree,
Dahling.
I won't hear of mere time clocking her down,
I won't.

And it's back to the box,
where she and I are strong and right
in sharp, stark, black and white
and we depart, because we've victories to win.

And Henreid waits with twin cigarettes.

► I stood at the shrine of Our Lady of Consolation Minor Basilica in Carey, OH, and touched remnants of miracle. Dozens of crutches and braces and stretchers were left behind by pilgrims who came to pray to the Virgin Mary. Apparently, she answered some of the prayers, and the faithful left their walking instruments as testimony to her good graces.

I used to be Catholic. But the laws of the church don't speak to me, never have, never will. I'm a heretic of the highest order, and I flaunt it.

THE GODDESS STRIKES AGAIN

But there was something comforting here.

As a work of the church, I couldn't buy it. I mean, the whole purpose of the church is to institutionalize mysticism, which is impossible.

You can't court magic through guilt.

Yet, out here in the middle of nowhere, was a shallow sigh of relief, an inconsistent little pocket of miracle that proved us wrong. A world without mystery had a heavy dose of pixie dust tossed in its face.

And I knew who was behind it.

It was the earth goddess.

Oh sure, the church said it was the Virgin Mary, but let's face it, the Virgin is nothing more than the goddess scrubbed of her pagan joy and demoted slightly.

We forget, she was the power of powers when the church was a mere glimmer of glamour in a rabbi's eye. Worshipped by millions in a thousand tongues under a hundred names. Kissing blessings on the desperate in a perfectly random manner, punishing the deserving and undeserving alike. True beauty indulges in as much bitchy whimsy as it wants. A miracle here, a healing there . . . would anyone like a bon-bon?

The church can think what it likes.

After all these years, she's still out there.

Having it all.

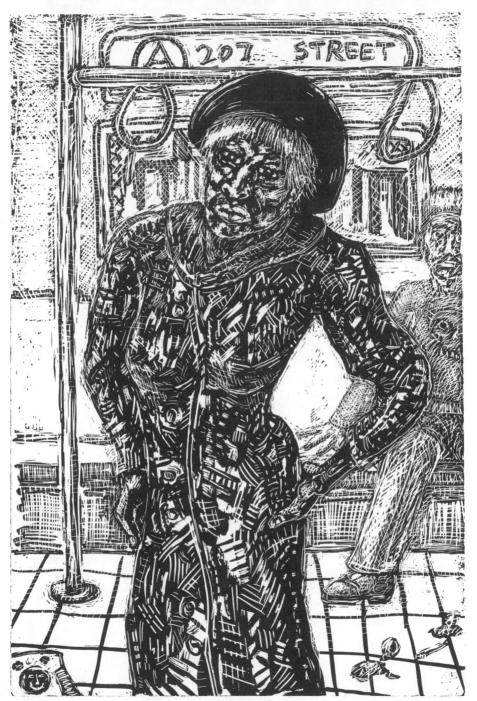

Home

► She's an ordinary overlook,
plain, brown meld
not worth a twice-glance, not once.
She's god's get-by, nature's slide,
she is as all.

But she opens a rough mouth,
which bleaches into the rest of her face,
hewn to be trivial,
you just know,
and rings the living bitter.

HOME

Heart with a direction
that winds and swirls
and wraps itself up in a thick, cream coat
of vision and gift.

She's hungry,
which is synonymous with fine
in fine art.
She can't lie,
she lacks the reserve
and so they hear.

Day-weary heads snap around
in this cool tomb of an underground ride
and here's pride.
Sure stance, iron spine.
Imagine that.

And there's a dead-time silence
as they step aside for spun-silver blessings.
She's noble.
Oh, she owns noble.
She's moon with that ice light.
Cold.
Cold, and truth-kissed clear.

And soon the hat's full and the stomach's not,
so she stops and blends and is as all.
But her eyes,
her eyes reign of knife-blade life denied,
for a while anyway.
The eyes say
try me.

▶ Because of the blues men,
their sad, black fire bridging for healing,
riffing for touch,
singing sickness is woman alone,
the child inside said fix it.

Because of the rockers,
making so much green off the African marriage,
telling her since she was fourteen
what she needed,
woo-mahn,

M ODERN LOVE

way down inside,
the rhythm in her said ride.

But because of the old poets mostly,
the ones who warned of withering,
of saddle-bag breasts and useless wombs
and the terror of no past to last
through a future alone,
the time inside said hurry.

And because she already knew the late night slides,
sweet on sweet,
she and he heating for just that one communion,
but stopping short,
because he was good and smart,
unfortunately.
With those silken failures in mind,
she looked to pass on the mantle but quick.

So she forgot her body,
which she never trusted,
forgot her mind,
which just got in the way,
forgot she was Catholic,
which came in handy.

And found him
someplace mindless, faceless,
found him
breezing with the casual she needed,
found him
looking like one serious clitoral chuckle,

And went with the minus.
Minus the time
when he tucks an invisible wisp behind your ear,
minus a brush of breath,
when he looks and doesn't,
and looks and doesn't
as if you, my girl,
are all the soft there is.
Minus that, she went,
screaming carpe diem, carpe diem.
And after she'd seized the deal,
she sat back and took a look
at what she'd learned.
A handful of logistics,
the surprise of burning,
non-momentum,
non-momentous,
non-moment.

And it was almost pitiful
the lack of force
with which she uttered
her most unimpressed
oh.

▶ She carries with her
a warm, harsh memory
reminding her of a night's stretch,
giving to gravity
built on the fire of repetition,
ending with a fold a sand.

He followed every outline her body could make.
A thousand, soft small kisses
given to god's hollows
a full tongue to the whole length

SCRATCH

of her spine.
Pausing at the base, cheeks to ass
to remind her that she was
undeniably sacred.
Lips to breast, sucking round,
showing her what she was and
what she could be as she grew inside him.

She bit every exclamation, every coercion.
If he knew that thick smile
that pointed push
that thin toothy wind
was approval,
well, there would be no dealing with him then.
And every love must have its leverage.

But there was no room
for that filling
no room for that joy
that pushed her head back
the pressure that settled into her chest
and the back of her throat.

She must divide and mark,
must slice and persuade,
the fine-laced muscles of her neck
dictated that she write a history
of grit and clench,
render portraits of screams.
Her thighs tightened around his waist
as her hand raked across the covering
that brought her there in the first place.

Her nails making home
in his skin, forcing it to follow and fall,
calling red flecks that
traced the arch of a talon.
His lips whistled an intake of breath,
his eyes rounded and brightened surprise,
as she mopped his loss discreetly
with her mouth.

▶ Sometimes
When I'm with him
like that,
I flashback
to tv movies,
Linda Blair,
"Born Innocent,"
the shower scene.
I'm thinkin'
she's havin'
more fun

SEX TALK

with prison pals
and the push
of an unlubricated broomstick
than I'm havin'
with him.

I says honey,
I'm the majority,
Cosmo's 90 percent,
the clitorally orgasmic woman.
He says honey,
that will have to change.
I says honey,
this ain't no
either/or,
cash or charge,
Cubs or Sox,
I ain't no two-scoop treat.

He says
wimmen in pornos
in Sweden,
those wimmen
anyway,
anyhow,
up the butt,
you could learn . . .

I'm thinkin'
my hand's
looking better
all the time.

for Pete and Elyn

▶ This is not about knots.
This is not about silken ties,
or rice or cake or wine.
This is not about bells or roads or rings.
This is not about once-worn clothes,
or the loss of veils and flowers.
This is not even about heaven
because your decisions and faults are earthly.

This is about smelly hockey gear

W HAT THIS IS

and filthy frying pans
and the patience it takes
to get around both of them.

This is about mornings when she's Godzilla
and the days when he's anal
and the nights when you must step away
or you'll scream.

This is about time
and how it molds love
like blown glass
that shatters if cooled too soon.
Keep your heat and breath strong.

This is about light
and how the brightness of love
might show you a life that
you only dreamed of seeing
once
before
alone.

This is about comfort.
Of taking his pain into yourself,
of hands at her shoulders ready to help,
of falling deep into your peaceful bed,
of reminding one another
when the night is cold
it's alright
it's okay
it's alright.

► Comes a time
when his lips stretch thin,
shambling over half apologies,
and he is speaking of traveling back
to the distance between you;
when eyes offered stuttering contact,
and the soft of his neck
is a means to an end,
and not an assumption itself.

SYNAPSE

Comes a time
in furrowed air,
when he qualifies sweetness
and reasons its waning;
and those purposely empty hands
clutch and gulp the air
waiting for dispensation,
and those eyes tunnel loss,
and look to you as thief.

Comes a time
when the chill hangs low and cold,
any and all holds are dismantled,
and together you're left
to grope your way down
from the easy levels you've assumed.

It is that time
when you freeze a full throat in pain,
count the pulses of your aching,
and wish somehow
that you were somewhat more
of a gift.

▶ He feeds her
with a lip to vulva instinct
she hasn't known since
oh
Friday.
And she with her slip-time smile
takes her tasty catch-all phrasing,
aches it all the way on back
and gives the boy something to point for.

The muscles of his back map reaction
as she grates nails

A NIGHT IN VIXENVILLE

across the tight protest of his ribs,
lulls sweeps in the sweet of his neck,
and mouths lessons in holes
best left excused.
They chafe to a grind,
smooth to please,
and shackle down
to clean, juice rhythm.

And he
blue milk arch
and he
full-throat stretch
and he
tension desperate
senseless and sense full
gaping wordless burning edge . . .

And he
he looks to her
for second salvation
yet another skin-lined redemption.

And she
ace dreamer
And she
queen cat
She blesses the prerogatives now counted among
her finest riches
as she says,
"Of course.
Stand in line."

▶ We sat in the murmurs of late,
giving each other victories,
the ones we always knew,
and had proven with time.

We spoke of power
we hadn't counted on.
When impact measures tense
in the muscles of his hands,
when snap and teeth take their place in deliverance,

FIONA AND I DISCUSS THE LOGISTICS OF FUCKING

when the ones who don't make noise
do.

We spoke of need,
which became central bleeding,
when slapping down a full-fist melancholia
is the hour's order
and more often than not,
sting was the answer and not the byproduct
and we liked it.

Which surprised us.
Neither of us had planned on standing to burn.

▶ Tracing slits of swords,
passing hands into body-hot iron
staining holy, holy,
he probed for proof of pain certifying Christ divine.
Even then inquiring minds wanted to know.

The book says he found it,
found all he needed in the hull of a god-man
and took his title as duke in prince
serf to servant, the book says.

W HOLE LOT OF THOMAS

But the press has lied to us before.
And I wonder if it was enough
or if, with hands dripping,
he demanded to see the trap door
or looked for himself in hidden mirror,
told his friends fun's fun,
but quit it with this resurrection shit.

He's in the story to give it guard, I think.
Because the breadth of it,
the blindly frightening depth of it
looms huge and terrible.

That the laugh above
might just have sent us something we could use.
That just this rare, rare once
things might have been exactly as they seemed
and more.
It's not in our nature to take such greatness lightly.

He was our wall against the oft-promised pledge
of spring against the cloak,
watching now as we're cloaked over and over,
watching now as we place the mantle
on the shoulders of the richest, slickest pompadour,
crying the most crock,
clanging "Jaysus" in glass cathedrals,
Places empty of Thomas when we need him most.

▶ The difference between a rant and a prayer
lies only in position and delivery.
raising yourself to the skies,
facing either the biggest laugh
or the only great eye,
hands up and open in surrender or supplication
or fisted in the fiercest demand,
the voice modulated between a thick strangle
and the soft, humble hangtime of pleading.

You say the same thing.
You're looking for the end of pain,

A PRAYER

looking to strike the world or the unworldly
with your anger, with your weakness,
with your absolute and complete inability
to take this shit anymore.

Personally, I prefer prayer.
It's not that I know someone's up there
It's that I can't bear to think that there's not.
Prayer is the knot at the end of the rope
that keeps us from finally falling.
Prayer is the small tug at the robe of a myth
that always stands over your shoulder
with its comforting color
and irritating politics.
Prayer is small and tentative
and set against the whispering background of hope.
And so we pray . . .

You
rage-cropped father,
You
earth-stained mother,
You
flaming spirit,
You
laughing jackal,
You
rising bird,
You
knowing shadow,
You
inner being.

I won't kneel
that will bring me closer
to what defeats me now.

I won't bow
because I can't cower
in the face of a question.
But I can ask
and hear my plea flood the air
and take comfort in the fact
that I still have the strength
to want.

I am so tired.
Cliches about weight aside,
the world has nested on my shoulders,
settling down for a long winter's nap.
My life follows the coldest road,
dark and indifferent,
and quite happy to roll on without me.
And sometimes I feel like I'm the only rider,
and that rests in me so heavily
I can only sit down
and hope for a deep breath.
When I look to the light of the future
I see no bright goal
only that same road
that forgets the sound of my steps.
You
who know the true meaning of beyond,
You
who hold the lives of so many
in your strange justice,
You
who promise this life will be justified,
send some of that folky old narcotic my way,
can't ya?
And let me step back awhile.

I ask for peace,
I ask for patience,
I ask for health,
I ask for truth,
I ask for beauty,
I ask for company,
I ask for love.

Amen
Omen
Whatever.

► Scream
Scream up heart,
scream up to this privilege,
cup and cradle dear,
because you must not waste it,
not one drop.

Here
Here you drive for distraction,
here you plead a golden moment in a brazen whole,
because you've always known this fist,

N

and you'll use it.

Stand
Stand foot safe and full,
stand territorial creator,
because this jam is yours now,
make no mistake.

And you're the one:
cool as roses,
bright as noon,
pointed like a dog's smile,
timelier than love,
sadder than the last man,
angrier than god roil,
saltier than sea sweep,
and sweet, and sweet, and sweet and sweet . . .
and silence packs your ears like cotton,
humming in to that one moment,
that one, lovely precious beat
when truth fuses,
time holds,
and they WAIT for you.
For YOU.
And the air splits with contact,
all you'll ever need.

Drink,
Drink high and clear,
drink deep and stay humble,
for it may never come again.

▶ The faces that glow down or out from media screens,
narcotic pieces of light,
do not count.
They play puppets to the story;
slack, parroting mouths waiting for other minds
to heighten their frenzied beauty.
They're a call with no response.

The faces that master any playing field,
fast champions,
do not count.

W HAT COUNTS

They are measured in points and percentages,
hard bodies steeled beyond a subtle touch.
Their heat moves them in a two-time cadence,
hotter than the lull of any wee-hour chat.

The faces we pay to carry our political administerings,
lie-low smiles,
do not count.
Their view is distant and diluted,
crowded with a clutter of pleas and deals.
Their sight extends to the next hand's press
and when they'll leave that warmth behind.

What counts
is looking so deep into your eyes,
that the color of the iris
never, ever escapes me.
Light draining down into wells of focus,
wet and unfazed;
a gaze honed finely to my attention's point.

What counts
is an ear open to all my life
like a lover;
to the foolish whole with all of its flaws.
Sifting through the lies and truths
until all that's left is gold.

What counts
is the voice that marries and divorces yours
at just the right times;
thrusts and retreats with its feedback

and acts as the vocal reminder
of the high pure solace
of true company.

What counts
is gathering in the primitive ways,
when the word pulsed with chord and timbre
and peace hung on inflection and presence;
circling on history's fire,
roaring with the warmth of living;
hearing the blood and memory that binds us,
binds us still,
and sharing your day at arm's length.

You, my friend;
I have life
I have time
for you.

Jangle

▶ She held promise like a stuffed toy,
in an inconsiderate childhood headlock.
It sugared her mouth,
and dribbled thick through her fists;
It flecked her eyes,
and gilded her laugh
as she slapped her black patent leather Mary Janes
against her grandmother's linoleum
and she didn't even care
if she made marks.
She was four.
And she was winning.

J ANGLE

Because she could, you know.
Bleed to please,
she worked it.
That child's own charm,
that bright-time sweep,
held such a sweet-lipped court,
such a fresh-day love
that you hoped and prayed
she never, ever was what she mirrored.

And behind her,
her parents cooed their euphemisms:
special, rare, unique.
This is what difference is,
they said.
Difference is everything.
Master it now for it is the sole criteria
through which others will judge you later.

Imagine her confusion, then
when the doctors in their white decisiveness
began to illustrate her failure.
Her engaging,
endearing,
off-kilter, puppy-dog lollop,
was translated into awkward and wrong.
They tickled her back with black felt-tip pens,
marking the places where her spine bent illegally.
They spoke to her parents of damaged brain cells

swimming in empty synapse,
and therefore of muscles
withering with a lack of information.
They said difference,
wrapped it in failure,
and placed it in her parents' lap.

To her parents, failure was everything.
She was their gift in many ways,
but she was also their creation
and if the creation was flawed
it would be fixed.

They sent her to a physical therapist.
His name was Ty and he had blue eyes
and bad breath.
He was fond of saying athletic things
like "no pain, no gain,"
and he made her tell him jokes
as he stretched her muscles
in places that her brain never told them to go.

Once
in an attempt to revive
motion and movement,
in an attempt to re-establish connections long since severed,
Ty wheeled out a black box on a metal cart.
He raised her pant leg,
and swathed her calf in conductive fluid.
It was cold
and itchy,
like most medical things,
but she didn't mind because

her Mu SCLe s qUivERed Ang RILY
WITH *the* shock
wave.
thE new force i n SIDE of her
AngERed *the* living
and WOK e the dead
FROM
thEIR LIQ u i d Slu MBer.
SPARki ng BL uE j*angle.*
CR a cK *ragged* tentacles
WHipPED their *un*FAM iliar WAY
UP HER CALF
br aNding HER *freak,*

AND anx *iety* AND *anger* s hot up HER sp *ine*
BURn ing her *freak,*
And IT shi vered *and* stung
as HER eye s TEAred and H ER throat FIL L ED

and she shouted,
no
you take it back
take it back
I don't like it
please

And she knew now.
This is what difference brings.
Difference in this world
is to bow, to bend, to break,
to fold your face and shade your heart.

And she knew now
that these were the lengths
that people would go to
to show her
that there really was no one like her
in this world,
and there never would be,
not if they could help it.

And she knew now.
This is what difference brings.
Difference is everything.

for Cindy Salach

▶ It will always be like this.

When we finally fit the key
and unlocked cages of words,
when we began to fashion the phrases
that chained our burdens to the world,
when we were chosen the cup
of some creative divinity's grace,
we knew we were on to something.

TO BE HEARD

We cut and buffed every facet of life
for the crowds to wear as they wished,
offered hands filled with the fat fruit
of our imaginations.
We skated on straight lines
that reached the point faster
than modern geometry would allow.

And the drink they filled our lips with
quenched us in its wash.
"I liked it,
you made me cry."
Poets don't live on this libation alone,
but let me tell you,
it goes really well with a burger.

And now that's our milk.
And quite frankly,
it's never known a better mother.

And that's why it hurts
when we're pushed back to the way it was:
when we face the tight, dark places
where the light doesn't catch like it should;
when all the perfect pictures spin out of our mouths
like clouds
and disseminate;
when our patience is smacked and laughed at;
when our voices are thrown back
like vicious spit balls;
when the air in our lungs is mopped up and wrung out.

And we know
that beyond all the progress we'll ever make
somewhere,
sometime,
it will always be like this.

Someone will always cut us with dismissal,
and begin to rebuild the walls
that we tore away
to enable us to do this in this first place.

But film to film,
trace to trace,
the scar tissue thickens
around our hearts
and braces them for breaking.
Rip and heal,
tear and heal.
And what once made us bleed profusely
dries as soon as it rises.

It will always be like this.
But what we leave in trying
is the legacy of
Effort.
And that's a very sweet word.

Scream on.
Next time
it won't hurt so much.

► It's a long way for educational take-out
but the Great White sweeps down from the North,
chords trained for games,
she slashes and dashes in all the right places.
It's hot then,
but she doesn't know it.

Seoul rises from ashes,
grey ghost of modern Korea,
Reeking with order
and lines and order,

VAL CONQUERS KOREA

and boxes and order,
and order,
and order.
It's hot then, but she can't see it.

Among the angles,
she finds her circle.
Round-eyed and rare,
they cling together for a little western warmth,
reveling in sake and unique.
It's hot then, but she won't do it.

One day she buys a Yes album
which was nothing like she knew it to be.
All uplift spirited away
like those who will not know the sanctioned songs.
And because she's the best of the west,
she's opportunity,
and when the outcasts come knocking,
she answers.
For that she's tailed,
and her mail is opened
and she's sweating.

And when a fellow student washes ashore
with a tear gas canister pin
embedded in her forehead,
it's soup,
and she's in it.

And breaks to a boil one day on campus
the air is seasoned with pepper gas,

She's breathing glass
and she runs and hides
and watches how it's played.

Waves of straight black onyx,
diamond eye,
absurdly rehearsed method madness.
The students ragjag with surgical masks.
They will lose no more of their own
and they will not take what's offered them,
thank you
and that's their order.
The cops are armored Darth Vader spawn.
They may agree with their enemy,
but all they see now is
youth and breaking
and that's a dangerous combination.

And it's attack and retreat,
attack and retreat
demonstrative two-step,
graceful violence, formula confusion
and the big boys soon tire of chapter review
and they slam down one killer take-home.

Which the students fail.
And there's a girl from her economics class
looking bad and bloodless
And as if by cue,
mothers mewl murder, murder.

And even before the fire dies down,
clean-up begins
and anger is neatly
folded and tucked away for another day.
Because being who they are
they'll do it until they get it right.
Shit, she thinks.
Not only are they the new captains of industry,
they're building a better Kent State.

► I reached the bottom of a pint of Guinness.
You were there.
I was surprised to find you
until alcohol pulled up a stool and
sat its loose, rumpled butt
down next to me,
and demanded to show me snapshots
of what you were once
and what it has made you.

DULLED

Oh, you had your points.
You were the break of a whip crack,
the slip of light razor,
a pop of flint spark.
That sharp.
That bright.

Your intelligence wasn't a gift
but a victory,
the best prize
at the bottom of the toy bubble.
Your sarcasm wasn't option,
it was mandate,
Lesser mortals must suffer
so they did.
I danced back in conversation
because you had facts,
and you knew fraud,
and you could catch me cold.

I counted on you
to keep the issues hard and unforgiving,
to keep my pacing strident
in a life that catered
to a malleable spirit;
to keep my world in windows,
so I could look elsewhere
for comfort.

Who would have thought that time
would be so thick with you?

There is a delay now between
question and answer
not pensive,
just empty,
as if the tools that would forge
a steely response had dulled
or the memory that would
billow and wield its skills
had forgotten its lessons.
The film of your eyes
waters the cut of you
with unrelenting wear.
The wall that you welcomed
as a challenging vault
has become a resting place.

I brace for the push
from the mire.
I wait for the slap
to the new world.
I look for the ghost of a wink
that showed us such promise,
such treasure.

Where are you, man?
When will you return?

▶ Catch me glassy vapid,
catch me mooning wordless,
catch me offtime-focus,
know me blessed and blessed.

There I am:
discordant, nouveau hooligan,
arched hands skeening bitchy on a steamy guitar.
My days whore short-lived syncopation;
I beat a nasty fractured push.

DOWNTIME

There I am:
Spring-coiled, muscled-up graceful,
the fruit of playground's labor caught in coursing,
Gravity's bastard with no legitimate ties,
I fly, I stuff, two . . . two . . .

There I am:
Babylon's worldly window,
stilettos staccatoing out
blood sharp swivels.
Mouth and mind and timing to match,
I'd love to kiss ya but I just washed my hair.

Catch me slack-move stupid,
catch me maw-deep living,
catch me slow-break gaping,
Know me blessed and blessed.

▶ I must
if nothing else in my life
be right.

I stand full in it,
that balance
knots untangled or severed in wisdom,
numbers compiled cleanly,
precise course charted and followed.

Being right hangs in the loose muscles of my neck,
the equilibrium of an easy heart,

RIGHT

the sure foot of a solid climb.
Being right is measured,
tempered,
and even,
like spring-flat girls on balance beams.

Most importantly,
being right is respite
from what the rest of the world finds wrong.

Like when you're broken
and you know it.
You hunt for alternative motion
that escapes you,
the laugh is too loud and loose,
the energy is spastic and embarrassing,
And you are retard
asshole
jagoff
faggot
and what binds you to the physical world
is laughably weak.

It is then that right places a flat hand
in the middle of your back
and says, "breathe."
Right sits you down and says,
"Here's something.
Make 'em dream."
Right unwinds the perpetual
tangle of nerves the world
bends you to
and allows you to fly.

Albany is the capital of New York.
bliss
The symbol for water is H$_2$O.
heaven
Al Capone went to jail for tax evasion.
ecstasy

And all the slight smiles
on all the pallid faces
behind all the glasses in the world
should never be dismissed as smug.
Don't sell them short.
For they know nirvana.

► Wesleptwewokeweatewefuckedwesleptwewokeweatewe-
fucked . . .

DarlingIloveyoudoyoulovemedarlingIloveyoudoyouloveme . . .

IamamanIamamanlymanthemostmanlymanIam . . .

HEMINGWAY AFTERNOON

Closethomosexualclosethomosexualclosethomosexual . . .

Bullfightingbullfightingbullfightingbullfighting . . .

It was good.

▶ Fascism begins early
and small.
It has through the years
been enhanced and exaggerated
to the dark drama of cruel boots
crushing small, brave movements.
But in fact
its workings are subtle.

I met my destined rendezvous with fascism
in Mrs. Emory's fourth grade class.

T HESE BOOTS ARE MADE FOR WALKIN'

Gloria Emory was a perky girl.
Her powder-blue eyeshadow
smoked up to brown-penciled brows,
her frosted blond hair
flipped with a
"What's Marlo Thomas got that I haven't got" curl,
her carefully pressed polyester pantsuit
cuffed cleanly above
ding-dong ditchy, witchy black heels.
She was Nancy Sinatra with half the attitude
and a little less thigh.

She was neat.
All the kids said she was neat.
SHE said she was neat,
and she expected everyone else to be neat, too.
And so, in an attempt to enforce
her iron-heeled, angora-covered
vision of neatness,
Mrs. Emory
would knock over and dump out
any desk that didn't match her standards.

Any desk.
Every desk.
Usually, my desk.

I didn't understand it.
I had an order.
A loveably, eccentric bit of chaos
slap-dashed with a bit of pre-artistic frenzy;
a loony, loopy, goony, goofy,

head-in-the-air,
mind-in-the-clouds,
dog-ate-my-homework kind of sensibility.
It worked for me.
I got stuff done,
I got my A's,
my work was mine.

And as I bent down to gather
and smooth my interrupted structure,
I wondered:
Where was the respect for my spark?
Where was the willow's tension?
Where was the wisdom
that would hold my decisions at an arm's length
and see them for what they were?

I dream sometimes.
I dream of reaching back and standing tall.
I dream of rising above
the mark of the arbitrary hand.
I dream of wresting away
the yoke of the thick-tongued minion.
I dream of stepping proudly outside
lines and plans.
I dream of rising to the fullness
of my four-foot-eleven frame,
cocking back solid on my heels,
burning up at that Maybelline-clotted eye,
that lemon-curdled, Jean Nate face,
the sterile wind
of a two, two, two-mints-in-one-mouth
and saying
Bitch
if you touch my desk again,
I will rip out your uterus
and spare future generations
the terror of your spawn.

But I wake.
I wake and I find myself bending
to the same small issues
from the same small minds
in the same shamefully small world.
I wake

and it's cold

and every pencil has a point.
He called at twelve-oh-one,
the meeting is at three,
I saved the receipt,
the paper is white.

I wake and I dream
of the warmth
of the fire
of chaos.

▶ I don't remember my temper.
I don't remember when the muscles in my back
first began to curl in
and clamp down over my shoulders
with an ache so deep
I thought it might pass on through.
I don't remember when my pulse
paced just a little bit quicker,
when my blood showed itself
as close as it could in the color of my skin,
when my heart started knuckling

TEMPER

its way through my ribs,
throbbing a clean, staccato beat,
a fit so fierce it made me weak
and threatened to stop my breathing.

I don't remember when my throat
began to strangle my voice,
to thin and break it,
to squeeze its air and purpose
and bend it to trembling.
But it's here now,
here through the grace of age
or some other vindictive keeper,
and it frightens me.

The world is pocked with unreasonable moments
with no room for the gentle cross and wrap of diplomacy,
moments so full of a lack of option
that all you see is heat.
Your mind has already chosen its side
and that's all that it will know.

My brain crackles with fantasies
of revenge against perpetrators
that are completely beyond my true abilities.
A smack to the bridge of the nose driving bone into brain;
Thumbs side by side,
pressing,
pressing,
closing a wind pipe.
Meeting out justice just as if
I were the only one who could

tear away the blindfold
and balance the scales.

And what's worse
this is a thing that will not be satisfied.
The light of the flashfire sweeps on.

People who stare at handicapped kids,
dilapidated schools in need of lottery money,
men who can't let a woman walk by quietly,
the entire Republican party,
police with cattle prods,
anyone who wears a swastika,
evangelists who feed on anything with faith,
religions that imprison their women,
our brand-new, can-do spirit,
wars with no forethought and no aftertaste
that are cheered on
like a fucking football game.
It builds within me,
feeds on the world,
and it will never,
ever
be quelled.

▶ My mother is very direct. That's why we're friends.

Once, while drunk on maternal recognition of my maturity, I slipped on a casual reference to some collegiate bedhopping I'd done. I figured, hell, she was just Catholic, she wasn't dead. I expected some kind of motherly admonishment because she's into that, but she just looked at me. And then she said:

"Lisa, I spent two weeks watching your uncle die of AIDS. We got there at the very end when he was at his very worst. Once, I remember a nurse was putting a breathing tube down his throat, and she said, 'Does it hurt? Are we in pain?' And he shook his

COUNTING

head no. But when I asked him, I said: 'John, are you okay? Does it hurt?' He shook his head yes and closed his eyes and went with it, because that's all that any of us could do, really.

And when it looked like he was going to be on a respirator permanently, we got together as a family and we gave him two weeks and I sat there in that hospital room and I said:

John
You've got two weeks left, honey, you better pull out of it . . .
John
You've got eight days left . . .
six days . . .
four days . . .
You've got two days left, John . . .

Until we had to let him go.

And frankly, Lisa, I don't think that a little piece of latex is too much to ask for the sake of your body and your mother's peace of mind."

My mother's direct, boy. That's why we're friends.

▶ The drone of online
dulled a metal sweet sleep
that made it painless to mop up melted time
and wring it into dumpster number one.

For me, the machine was easy.
It asked for nothing but reaction
and acquiescence to rhythm.
Sky-high wages for steel-toed idle?
No problem.
So I moved with it.

SIRENS AT THE MILL

And after a while
it was breath,
it was beat,
brand-new involuntary.

And as I locked on into patterns,
all I could do was listen:
to blue-blade harmonies,
steel-braced downbeat,
repetita,
repetita,
repetita,
repetita
in knife time.
It was nice.

I numbed
and understood
how anyone could wear the grind
lifer with shard smile
because the whole thing is habit
and ritual
and there's no place safer.

And then
right in the middle of constant,
on top of rely,
right next to depend,
there's this catch

on a ring that I'm not supposed to be wearing.

There was time, I thought
for a laugh or two.

there was room, I thought
for a healthy
"well fool, look what you did now,"
I mean, there's always slack in my schedule.
Until I felt it:
the rip of penitence,
pinch of metal press,
crush of forward,
and old cliches stepped lively,
cold as a machine,
thorough as a machine.
And I thought of my brother
down at the popsicle factory,
put his hands on a guardrail
as a two-ton punch press
whistled millimeters from his fingers.
And I thought of my grandfather
down at the Coca-Cola bottler,
he lost half of both his thumbs,
and you wonder where these scars come from,
from here,
from now,
here and now,
here and now,
because it's not stopping,
it won't STOP,
and I can feel it pull absence of ice,
and itch of flame,
and the smooth, dry, crossgrain of a man's back,
and I know,
I know,
I know,
I know,
I know . . .

Until some slo-mo supervisor swam through nappy-time,
and pushed a button;
gave me back a sense of gift;
tangible grace now,
one under which we flourish,
and one that I will not now
do without.

Drive

▶ Daddy and me
we got a taste for something sweet.
It ain't where we are,
ain't that the way he says,
so we drive.

Daddy drives diagonally,
with his body at a fuck-off slant,
one arm straight out to the steering wheel
and the other slung over the seat,
his best girl.

DRIVE

He smokes and I wear his rings,
burps the alphabet and I giggle.
Me and him and Dinah Washington,
What a dif'rence a day makes. . .
Daddy likes them lush arrangements.

Sooner or later we find what we're looking for,
Michigan cherries at a roadside stand.
We eat them unwashed,
gleeful at how much that
would piss Mama off.
We spit the pits up through our custom deluxe sunroof,
planting cherry trees all over Northwest Ohio.

And I know these times are right.
I look at him and his forehead is smooth,
and I know for a couple of hours he feels
like he's going somewhere,
doing something.

And I don't have to worry
about the times when his eyes heat,
and his lips thin,
and he barks when he speaks.

And I don't have to worry
about the time
when he finds exits that I've never seen
and takes them,
and takes them.
It's then that I know,
then that I hope,
that I'll be enough to get home on.

▶ People don't die of just pneumonia now.
But they don't know that where I come from.
So when the slight and precise died
of the media's latest baby,
we lied,
and swept his immaculate life
out of the spotlight
with one clean statement.

Who could blame us, really?
The community saw the loss of a martyr,

10

but everyone else saw the unfortunately wayward,
and both offered socially responsible condolences,
but no one had a sense of the whole,
so screw it.
With a raincoat, of course.

When you're a kid,
the biggest sin you commit is political ignorance.
We knew nothing of rifts or chicer deviances.
To us, he was just
the hugger, the holder,
the kisser, the singer,
the maker, the reacher,
and when he left, we said
"When? When again?"

When I saw him on holiday,
it was like that theatrical make-up course I took,
when they taught us how to die.
Concentrate on the shadows, they said.
When I got there,
he was concentrating real hard.
All regular angles,
all planes and crevices,
clearly highlighted and defined.
The color of vitality is only perceptible when gone.
And I memorized that vacancy,
so that I'd know it
when it came to see me later.

So I thought I'd dance my liberal dance,
and tell him that it didn't matter,

that I was fine with what he was.
But then I figured it wasn't my space
to dispense forgiveness,
especially when it wasn't solicited.
And he left without due approval,
mine or his.

So then we said goodbye to him in a house that,
despite his allegiances and beliefs
didn't even want to know.
And through it all,
I laughed to him,
I said,
you asshole.
You're ashes,
and they're telling me
how well I've filled out over ravioli.

When again?

The bubonic.
Now there was a plague.
We killed ourselves then
because we were slobs,
and not because we were lonely,
or in search of a more direct hit.
It was the ultimate teenage nightmare:
clean up your room or go with roses.

Had the caution mongers been alive
during the Dark Ages,
what light could they have shed?
Hang with the clean rats?
Then as now
who can tell?

So we left him to the Atlantic coast.
The turbulent to turbulence.
My father and my uncle went to Boston's North End
to get what was left.
For Daddy,
anniversaries hurt, I think.

And the little old Italian ladies
who lived there stood
and watched
and shook
83   and clucked.

And one of them approached my uncle,
who had inherited this responsibility
through marriage and sheer golden character.
And she said,
"He had such style."
And my uncle said,
and we say,
"Yeah. You should have known him when."

▶ Nadine held my hand when we were kids.
When she stopped I thought she didn't love me anymore.

Can I braid your hair?

We used to call my grandma "the Hoover,"
because her kisses were like a vacuum.

I love you, a bushel and a peck, a bushel and a peck and
a hug around the neck . . .

When I lost my virginity in a less-than-romantic manner, Fiona
put the tea pot on.

M ISS MARY MACK

He's an asshole. Need a hug?

Val took me to the campus clinic. They had a VHF Viewmaster
that showed the pap smear process up close and personal.

Maybe we should tone it down a bit . . .

When her husband died, Mrs. Goldberg broke down over the
thought of going on their upcoming trip to Europe solo.

I held her. She felt small.

I lay in my mother's bed, it was her bed then,
and I told her I was ugly and nobody liked me.

My darling, you will always be beautiful to me.

▶ Somewhere between easy listening
and turn that shit down,
you find a middle ground,
and you watch your vehicle for being here
as she dances.
And you swear parenthood must suck
every bit of coordination from the human body.

'Cuz it's so sad.
She's doing this half-beat-back
Carmen-Miranda-tropical-cha-cha thing,

PATSY ROCKS

and you are reminded
that for 51-year-old, white Irish Catholic women
rhythm is a figment of the imagination.

But as she ponies over the gold shag,
it hits hard that you weren't always
an integral part of her plans.
And all of her unknown life stands up
and demands to be counted.

Look again
and time shakes away clean:
She's 18 now and she loves an Italian boy
she met at a wedding,
S.W.A.K.
T.L.A.
and she's dancing

And she's 20, 24, 28 with babies,
packs up her faith and moves to strange places
but she's dancing

And the life isn't quite what was promised by someone.
And the kids can be so vicious sometimes
she hadn't imagined that.
Parents pass away,
and something breaks for her everyday,
but damn, she doesn't miss a beat.

And it's beautiful.
Right there in front of you,
utterly failing to shake a tailfeather,
is continuity.

And it's beautiful
because despite everything
that's been given her,
she still knows what it is
that makes her move.

And in the face of that,
all you can muster from
your too-hip-to-live lips is
Go, ma.
Alright.